Table of Contents

INTRODUCTION ....

Chapter 1: The Fundamentals of Mindfulness and Scientifically-Proven Benefits for Health 4

Chapter 2: The Importance of Brain Transformation Before Body Change 10

Chapter 3: Negative Body Image and Change of Negative Beliefs 14

Chapter 4: Do Your Thoughts Make You Fat? 20

Chapter 5: The Stress and Metabolism Connection 27

Chapter 6: Relaxation and Burning Calories 30

Chapter 7: The Psychology of Eating 33

Chapter 8: Binge Eating, Compulsive Overeating, Emotional Eating 38

Chapter 9: The Implications of Hormonal Imbalances 44

Chapter 10: Happy Exercise vs. Stress Exercise 49

Chapter 11: Mindful Eating 54

Chapter 12: Mindful Breathing 58

Chapter 13: Mindfulness Mini Habits for Weight Loss 62

Chapter 1: Practical Mindfulness Exercises – Step-by-Step Easy to Follow Mindfulness Routines to Lose Weight 69

Chapter 14: Losing Weight – What Works and What Doesn't Work (Debunking Myths) 75

Chapter 15: Optimizing Your Results with Supplements, 7 Minute HIIT 78

Chapter 16: Balancing Your Hormones 84

Chapter 17: Great Nutrition Strategies that Will Speed Up Your Metabolism.. 88

Chapter 18: Healing Nourishment 91

Chapter 19: Building Lifelong Mindfulness Habits 94

Chapter 20: 10 Steps Mindfulness-Based Program that Will Melt off Fat Forever 99

CONCLUSION 103

MINDFUL EATING

How to Stop Binge Eating and Overeating, Lose Weight Permanently and Forever Heal Your Relationship with Food

(Mindfulness Book Series, Book 3)

BY

SARAH JONES

© Copyright 2017 by Sarah Jones

All rights reserved. No part of this book may be reproduced in any form without permission in writing from the author. Reviewers may quote brief passages in reviews.

Disclaimer

No part of this publication may be reproduced or transmitted in any form or by any means, mechanical or electronic, including photocopying or recording, or by any information storage and retrieval system, or transmitted by email without permission in writing from the publisher.

While all attempts have been made to verify the information provided in this publication, neither the author nor the publisher assumes any responsibility for errors, omissions, or contrary interpretations of the subject matter herein.

This book is for entertainment purposes only. The views expressed are those of the author alone, and should not be taken as expert instruction or commands. The reader is responsible for his or her actions.

Adherence to all applicable laws and regulations, including international, federal, state, and local governing professional licensing, business practices, advertising, and all other aspects of doing business in the US, Canada, or any other jurisdiction is the sole responsibility of the purchaser or reader.

Neither the author nor the publisher assumes any responsibility or liability whatsoever on the behalf of the purchaser or reader of these materials.

Any perceived slight of any individual or organization is purely unintentional.

INTRODUCTION

Are you aware of what you eat? Do you taste each mouthful and chew it thoroughly before swallowing? Are you in control of your eating habits, or do you eat even when you're not really hungry, using food as a way of coping with unpleasant emotions of stress, anxiety, sadness, anger, frustration, or simply emptiness?

If you're reading this book, it is possible that you've been trying hard to shed pounds, and despite that effort you haven't yet seen permanent positive changes in your physique. You've started to think that perhaps you didn't find the right diet, or that you don't have enough willpower, and therefore you need to try harder or simply start again. And you did it. Again, and again, and again, before you realized that it wasn't just you. So many other people around you were doing the same thing and it didn't work for them either. After yo-yo dieting for years, you went back to the same eating habits and the same beliefs that you're a failure and that it is impossible for you to lose weight. The same old frustrations took charge and, as a result, your self-esteem went into another downward spiral.

Many people have now realized that being fit, healthy, lean, and brimming with energy isn't just about dieting or spending hours in the gym. Research shows that the main reason you turn to food, binge, overeat—and, as a result, put on weight—is that you don't have better ways of managing your life's ups and downs, daily stresses and emotional challenges. You treat food as a medicine and painkiller. You regularly deprive yourself, succumb to temptation, feel guilty, and then start the process again.

If you want to break this vicious cycle forever, you need to learn effective life skills. With those skills, you won't need to turn to mindless eating to make it through the day. You will be able to take care of yourself physically and emotionally, and create a passionate and meaningful life. With those skills, food will regain its proper meaning: being nourishing and joyful at the same time. You won't have to diet and starve yourself to death and your weight will naturally go back to a healthy norm. Eating will become one of many life's pleasures again!

Mindful Eating provides simple and proven strategies that will allow you to enjoy eating foods that you love without fear, guilt, or binging—and help you create the healthy and vibrant life you deserve. It will also help you to rebuild your relationship with food and show you exactly how you can establish proper dietary habits to lose weight naturally and healthily. We will shed light on some seemingly unrelated factors that actually prevent you from slimming down. You will discover how your thoughts, beliefs and small daily actions reflect your food decisions and the way you look and feel about yourself. You will explore the close connection between your daily routines, behavior and well-being.

Free your mind from the stress of being overweight and the futility of slimming diets. Learn the sweet taste of mindfulness to stop using food to solve emotional problems. Discover how to regulate your body weight without deprivation or calorie counting, turn your eating-autopilot off and avoid reacting blindly to difficult emotions. Learn how to distinguish between physical hunger and psychological hunger.

Mindful Eating emphasizes how mindfulness can heal your relationship with food and bring your awareness to the table so that you could taste the difference and allow yourself to truly enjoy it. You will understand how mindful eating and breathing can significantly change the way you think about food and your food choices. Through learning simple mini-habits and following proven nutrition tips you will experience much more freedom and joy when eating. We will tackle the myths surrounding weight loss, as well as find out which exercises will do more harm than good. Most importantly though, this book won't merely help you trim your waistline – it will transform your life.

There is so much more in store for you in this holistic approach to shedding pounds. Turn to the first chapter and begin your journey of personal improvement. Learn how to apply mindfulness antidote to ineffective dieting.

CHAPTER 1

The Fundamentals of Mindfulness and Scientifically-Proven Benefits for Health

Mindfulness refers to a state of active, open, and non-judgmental attention to the present moment. When you are mindful, you become observant towards your feelings and thoughts, without labelling them as good or bad. You live in the moment and stay awake to experiences. If this is your first time learning about mindfulness, such concepts may seem to be difficult to grasp at first. After all, you haven't yet learned about the mind and its roles –both positive and negative.

The Importance Within

As human beings, we tend to see things from an external perspective. For example, if we're faced with a problem, we typically focus on solutions that affect the things around us. While that comes with its own advantages, and is to an extent necessary, it is limited at best. To truly deal with dilemmas, we have to look into what's within the mind – we have to change how we perceive and understand reality.

In a way, all things exist simply because the mind itself acknowledges their existence. Perception begins within you, and so the existence of others actually begins with you. Note that we aren't trying to change your view of reality itself. Mindfulness is about knowing and paying attention to what's really happening – a perspective that's free of biases, undistorted by fears and expectations. Simply put, it is through mindfulness that you'll have a clear vision towards your goal.

Practice Fundamentals

Mindfulness encompasses everything. So even if your aim is to lose weight, appreciating your dining experiences by focusing on what can be "felt" by your taste buds won't be enough. To truly unlock its potential, you have to familiarize yourself with four foundations or fundamental aspects. And the first one is *mindfulness of the body*, which is all about achieving a sense of groundedness.

To understand that concept, you'll have to realize that most of us do not perceive the body in its simplest form. We tend to create projections and conceptualizations when we interact with our bodies, and when we use it to interact with objects. Being mindful of the body means that you're able to engage in a direct and pure activity. If you sit, for example, you really sit—you're aware of how the ground feels, you notice your breathing, and your mind is free of any judgements and opinions.

Mindfulness of life is the second foundation or fundamental. It's mainly centered on accepting the struggle (whether for survival or in any other challenges you may face) as proof of your existence—and as a necessary part of existence itself. In other words, by being mindful of life, you move through each day without clinging to distractions and without questioning everything. You don't need reassurance just to feel alive—you're alive because you are, and that is enough.

This is where the "touch-and-go" approach to mindfulness is most applicable. You don't have to continually ask why things are happening around you and desperately try to find answers. All you have to do is acknowledge the existence of whatever obstacles or challenges you are facing, see them in their purest sense, and afterwards let go of your focus and move on to other things – or, in other words, just continue living. It is through mindfulness of life that you will manage to turn the practice into an innate ability.

Now, the third of these fundamentals is *mindfulness of effort*. This isn't about giving it all you've got for the sake of achieving your goal. Remember that mindfulness primarily focuses on seeing things for what they are, and shifting your attention to whatever comes next. Effort, in the context of mindfulness, is doing what's natural. It's a sudden action without a defined objective or destination.

This leads to greater spontaneity and reduces the burden of each action. After all, instead of consciously steering yourself towards the objective and thinking about the reasons why you should be doing such a thing, you instead feel an invisible push or a sudden flash that simply leads you to act—and following that up with another act won't need much energy. Mindfulness of effort allows you to keep your wheels turning while eliminating unnecessary doubts and burdens.

Mindfulness of mind is the fourth and final entry in this list. It's similar to those we have discussed so far, in the sense that it's mainly about having a single-shot perception. It's about thinking at things one by one, at the most basic of levels. For example, instead of having all sorts of thoughts about the summer heat and how it's making you feel, you should just think and acknowledge that you're feeling hot and that you're sweating.

Knowing all these foundations, you should have a basic understanding of what mindfulness entails—and how it primarily works. It's also likely that you now have an idea of how it could help you in your quest for weight loss. It's perfectly fine if you're feeling a bit skeptical—but kind an open mind. As we will see in the next section, there are many scientific studies that prove the merits of mindfulness!

Benefits of Mindfulness

According to researchers at the University of New Mexico, practicing mindfulness can help reduce binge eating and anxiety. Employees who practiced mindfulness for twenty minutes a day were found to reduce their stress levels by 11 percent. Individuals with prostate or breast cancer were also found to improve their immune systems after eight weeks of practicing mindfulness.

Mindfulness has long been practiced for its mental health benefits. It is particularly recommended to people who are suffering from anxiety. A Massachusetts General Hospital study in 2013 that consisted of ninety-three people with generalized anxiety disorder (GAD) has revealed that practicing mindfulness can help reduce anxiety.

Mindfulness meditation can also reduce age and race bias. People generally depend on cognitive shortcuts and established associations. Some of these shortcuts are crucial, such as finding out what your bias is towards your preferences for meal times. Then again, such associations can also be destructive, particularly with regard to race and age.

In addition, mindfulness-based cognitive therapy (MBCT), which combines cognitive behavioral therapy (CBT) with mindfulness-based stress reduction (MBSR), can help prevent and treat depression. The American Psychological Association has found that mindfulness exercises, such as yoga and body awareness, can improve symptoms of depression.

Dr. Willem Kuyken from the University of Oxford claims that through mindfulness, individuals at risk of depression can more effectively recognize what is happening to them and deal with their issues with compassion and equanimity. In his study, he has proven that MBCT can help prevent the recurrence of depression just like antidepressants.

Moreover, mindfulness increases body satisfaction. Women are generally dissatisfied with their bodies. Researchers Kristin Neff, Karen Dill-Shackleford, and Ellen Albertson conducted a study in which female participants were assigned into two groups: the control group and the meditation intervention group. The participants in the intervention group had self-compassion meditation training for three weeks, while those in the control group did not have any training. After the study, it was found that the participants who underwent meditation training were able to increase their body satisfaction and self-worth.

Another benefit of mindfulness is improved cognition. In a study published in the Consciousness and Cognition Journal in 2010, it was found that mindfulness meditation can boost mood levels, increase mindfulness, and reduce anxiety and fatigue. Mindfulness training has also been found to improve working memory, executive functioning, and visual-spatial processing.

CHAPTER 2

The Importance of Brain Transformation Before Body Change

Many people are not aware that the mind is responsible for the development of the body. In other words, the transformation in your brain can have a significant impact on the changes in your body.

According to researchers at the University of California, there is a connection between abdominal fat and mindfulness in obese and overweight individuals. At the end of the study, which was conducted over four months, one of the participants was able to lose fourteen ounces of belly fat. In one year, she was able to lose twenty-five pounds and two inches from her waistline. No, she did not undergo any diet. She simply changed the way she thought about eating.

Dr. Jennifer Daubenmier states that the main idea behind the study was to tune in to the physical sensations of fullness, taste satisfaction, and hunger—as well as to eat depending on this particular awareness instead of stress. The participants of the study attended classes on mindfulness, where they were taught how to notice negative feelings and resist an urge to find comfort in eating.

The fat cells in the abdomen contain four times as many cortisol receptors as the fat cells in other parts of your body. So, when you get stressed out, the cortisol—which is your body's primary fight-or-flight hormone—binds to these cells and makes them store more fat. Your genetic makeup has evolved in ways that can be useful for your body. In this case, it is only useful for the short term. It allows you to store energy quickly for dangerous situations. However, it is not beneficial for you in the long run.

You have probably heard the saying "You are what you eat". While this is true, it is also true that "You are also what you think." This theory has been confirmed by researchers at the Norwegian University of Science and Technology (NTNU). Thousands of average weight teenagers aged thirteen to nineteen participate in their study—these participants were measured and weighed, and also asked questions regarding their body image and lifestyle.

Years later, the participants were examined again. During this time, they were already young adults between the ages of 24 and 30. The researchers found that those who thought of themselves as fat teenagers gained .88 body mass index units more than those who thought they were of normal-weight when they were teenagers. Koenraad Cuypers, a researcher on the project, hypothesized that by merely thinking of themselves as fat, they actually became fat.

The Science Behind "Fat Thoughts"

The University of Georgetown has published a study that shows how anxiety and stress trigger a body reaction that causes belly fat to develop. They found that when you are stressed out, your body produces neuropeptide neurotransmitters, which go to your belly fat cells and make them bigger.

Another reason why individuals who think that they are fat actually become fat is because their diets are affected by their thinking. They tend to eat foods that are low in fat as well as skip meals while they work out. If you do this, your body will only go back to its weight before you starved and overworked yourself. If your body is no longer able to keep up with your regimen, it becomes fat.

So how can you lose weight? Well, the first step is to change the way you think about yourself and your body. A change in your mindset can have a significant impact on your body. Instead of thinking that you are fat and that you have to starve and overwork yourself, think that you can reach a healthy weight by getting adequate amounts of sleep and nutrition. Visualize yourself as a healthy, slim and energetic person who only eats food that is healthy and nourishing. Create a mental picture of yourself as good-looking and slim. Do it every day, at least a few times a day.

Positive mental focus is essential to losing weight in a healthy manner. Rather than focusing on how much weight you have to lose, focus on how wonderful you feel about your body. See to it that you also congratulate yourself for making progress. This way, you will stay motivated to reach your weight loss goals. Remember that losing excess weight to reach your ideal weight is necessary, but you should never strive to be underweight.

You can break free from your fat thoughts by practicing visualization techniques, yoga, and mindfulness meditation. Visualization requires you to envision what you want to happen. Take note that your mind cannot distinguish between real and imaginary. Thus, you have to focus on what you want instead of what you do not want. Yoga involves gentle stretches that allow you to exercise and relax at the same time. Mindfulness meditation helps you stay in the present moment by letting go of anxious thoughts about the past and the future.

CHAPTER 3

Negative Body Image and Change of Negative Beliefs

In order to successfully apply mindfulness to losing weight, you need to first understand the importance of beliefs—and before that, you must learn what beliefs are. Beliefs determine how you perceive things. They define what is right and wrong for you, and thus, in turn, influence whether you feel good or bad about whatever it is that's happening. We can say that beliefs are your very own unique programming.

How do they work in practice? For example, if you're faced with someone who's starting to criticize your decisions, you might immediately try to come up with all sorts of ways to refute what's being said. Criticism is in conflict with your belief that you have to be right, or that you are always right and accepting a mistake will damage your credibility.

In the context of your body, or specifically your physique, negative beliefs may manifest in how you react to other people's comments. Here's one example—someone tells you that you seem to be gaining weight, and so you begin to starve yourself. This could also manifest without involving others. Let's say you believe that dropping two sizes should give you the body you desire, but despite working hard you failed to realize such a goal. In effect, you ended up feeling down.

From Belief to Negative Image

Sadly, many people tend to harbor negative beliefs, and these negative beliefs affect their body image. Your mindset develops from your life experiences. Even though some of them may have served you well in the past, they will not necessarily serve you well again in the future. Consider the following questions:

- Do you think that you will stay fat no matter what you do?

- Do you think that your genes fully determine the way your body looks, so you cannot do anything about it?

- Do you think that you are not committed and disciplined enough to be in the shape that you desire?

If you answered 'yes' to these questions, then your mind—and the beliefs that you have about what is possible for you and what is not—is preventing you from losing weight and reaching your goals. If you think that you are fat and don't believe that you can change, then you are going to be fat. If you think that you do not have the capability to lose weight, you will not lose weight. If you do not change your way of thinking, you will not be able to change anything permanently. You will keep reaching for another "miracle diet" and end up frustrated that it didn't work again.

Failing to achieve what you perceive as the right physique (or failing to adopt positive beliefs soon enough) can eventually lead to a negative body image. While this may not seem too alarming, note that people who experience it are considerably more dissatisfied with themselves—each time they look in the mirror, they only see what's wrong. They focus on specific parts of their body being bigger or smaller than necessary. As a result, they often lack self-confidence, suffer from stress, anxiety and depression. All of that prevents them from living a truly happy and fulfilled life.

Shifting to Positive Perception

You now understand how your negative body image influences your life and how harmful it can be for your desire to lose weight. You are also aware that the negative beliefs you hold have kept you from achieving the fitness level and body shape you crave. So, it is time to change old beliefs and replace them with more positive ones that will serve your goals.

To do that, you must know the difference between the kinds of beliefs that lead to a negative body image and those that reinforce a positive body image. Here's one good example—a friend of yours believes that the only way to look good is to have a supermodel frame, while you believe that you look good as long as you feel strong and healthy.

Now, your friend's belief could be impossible to achieve even after exerting considerable effort (genes play a role in this, after all). That means it's likely that she will only get frustrated and begin to hate her body. You, on the other hand, know that you're not really in peak condition and that there's room for improvement—but since you appreciate your good health and you have sufficient strength, you don't end up hating your body. You appreciate it more with every bit of improvement, whether from working out or from eating properly.

Here's another belief that leads to a negative body image: beauty is defined by how others see you. And of course, the opposite of that is accepting yourself for what you are and appreciating how you look.

It won't be hard to imagine how the first belief could be harmful to a person—after all, there's no guarantee that others criticize objectively. There's a chance that even if you've achieved that supposedly perfect physique, you'll still garner criticism from envious individuals. Alternatively, if you accept yourself completely (without dismissing the advantages of slimming down), what others say won't affect you—and you won't be bound by society's definition of beauty.

Changing with Daily Practice

Beliefs can be good or bad, beneficial or harmful—and you can change bad ones through some simple exercises. The body scan (which is a popular mindfulness technique) is an excellent example of such an exercise, as it allows you to appreciate your different parts and helps you establish that much-needed link between mind and body. To do it, simply follow these steps:

- Go somewhere quiet and relaxing. Sit down comfortably.

- Close your eyes and take a few deep breaths.

- At this point, notice your feet as they touch the floor. Feel the sensations.

- After a short while, move up to your legs. Note their every aspect.

- Once you're done, it's time to shift your attention towards your back.

- Continue to move from one part to another until you reach your head.

- Finally, pay attention to your body as a whole.

- Take a deep, relaxed breath and then open your eyes.

While the daily mindfulness exercise might seem simple, it gives you the chance to realize that your body has unique and interesting qualities—and that there's nothing wrong with it in the most basic sense. Try to practice this daily and soon your beliefs will shift from criticism and comparison towards appreciation and acceptance. If you would like a more detailed and conscious approach, however, try this exercise instead:

- Write down all your body-related beliefs.

- From everything that you've listed, pick the one with the greatest impact.

- Now, think about the ways that this belief has proven to be harmful.

- Imagine that a friend of yours has this belief.

- Do your best to come up with arguments that invalidate the belief.

- Of course, try to imagine his comebacks and respond accordingly.

- Once you're done, come up with an opposite positive belief.

- Imagine that you've held this belief for quite some time.

- Visualize how things are better with this beneficial mindset. See it and feel it in your mind.

- Do that as you wake up and go to sleep in the next few days.

You can further reinforce this exercise by coming up with a list of ways in which you could disprove the harmful belief. Write down two to three daily, and do your best to actually do them the next day. Being mindful of how incorrect your views are keeps you grounded in reality. It lets you avoid illogical tendencies and prevents your baseless fears and worries from controlling your life—or in this case, your body image.

CHAPTER 4

Do Your Thoughts Make You Fat?

Thought patterns play an important role when it comes to losing weight. No, this isn't just about thinking that you're fat and eventually (or inevitably) gaining weight—we've covered that in the previous chapter. The thoughts that we are going to discuss here are much more general in nature, meaning they aren't necessarily related to food or weight. What's common among them, however, is that they all lead you to engage in pound-gaining activities.

Fattening Thought Patterns

Any negative thought pattern (or, in other words, negative thinking) can make you fat. How? Well, the kind of mentality that constantly brings you down also limits your self-control. It prevents you from making sound decisions, leading to actions that you'll surely regret afterwards. Does that make you remember something? Yes, there are lots of poor decisions to be made when you're surrounded by food—after all, it's capable of giving you temporary pleasure.

If you're having a difficult time understanding this concept, it's probably best to look at some examples of these detrimental thoughts.

- I'm a failure, and no one will ever like me.

- I made a mistake. I can't do anything right.

- Someone's angry again. What did I do this time?

- He's not paying attention to me. I'm not attractive.

- I'll never amount to anything. She will always be better than me.

- I made a mistake. Surely, I have already ruined this entire pursuit.

- I've done something wrong so I might as well continue making mistakes.

It's practically guaranteed that once any of those thoughts enter your mind, you would end up feeling bad—and other similar thoughts will begin to pop up and linger, making you feel depressed and worthless. That's the point where you'll seek instant gratification, which, in most cases, will be in the form of food. Also, healthy food doesn't typically grant an immediate release of endorphins. Sweet, sugary sweets are the prime choice.

Changing the Way You Think

How do you change negative thought patterns? You could either tweak them or add to them. Tweaking is actively believing the opposite of your thought, saying it out loud with a smile on your face and a strong conviction—daily or whenever negative thoughts begin to creep in. Let's start with an example: "I'm not attractive." To nullify that, acknowledge your own unique beauty and say: "I'm beautiful in my own special way!" Say it with confidence and smile on your face (a smile costs nothing and is very powerful). Say it as if your life depended on it. Paint a picture of yourself being beautiful, unique and brimming with energy. It may sound foolish and odd at the beginning, but trust me, it really works. Just make a decision to do consistently.

The second approach is easier to do for those who are accustomed to having negative thought patterns. Let's use this thought pattern as an example: "I made a mistake. I can't do anything right." When you notice that you've said that in your head, simply add this: "…but that's impossible. I know I've succeeded many things before. As for this endeavor, I'll just have to do better to succeed." To reinforce this approach, keep a daily journal of your personal achievements where you will be writing down all the small and big successes you have. Make sure you have access to it whenever you are unhappy with your results. It will be your point of reference grounding you in the belief that you are *already* a successful person!

Here are some examples of small successes: "I managed to get up 10 minutes earlier today and read an inspiring book," or "I went to the park and spent 5 minutes being present and enjoying everything around me". Bigger successes might be: "I finished the project that is very important for my work," or "I raised two amazing kids," or "I've learned a foreign language and can now use it while travelling the world." Be creative with it. Search for all the possible successes you've already had. Don't be intimidated. I am sure you've had many successes. Just dig in your head and you'll be able to find them. Perhaps you've never done that before and that's why nothing comes to your mind at first. Don't be discouraged. Keep thinking and write it down.

Harmful thought patterns are essentially baseless. They magnify your fears and worries, and they eclipse your true worth and capabilities—if you let them. Fortunately, there are ways to rewire your mind. Finding the right approach is as easy as reflecting on how you think. If you're the visual type, for example, replacing the negative images formed by your thought patterns with encouraging ones will be easier to pull off.

Remember, make it a habit to observe your thoughts and uncover the ones that don't serve you. Think of all the possible positive aspects of your body that you are proud of and write them down. Keep the list somewhere close at hand, and look at it when you feel down or depressed. You've probably heard the catchphrase "Fake it till you make it." It means that you behave and think as if have already achieved you goal. In other words, imagine yourself as a slim, healthy, energetic person and act as if it was already true. To achieve that, ask yourself these questions:

- What beliefs would I have if I have already achieved my goal?

- What thoughts would I have?

- How would I walk and speak?

- What would my body language be like? How would I stand? How would I walk? How would I speak and breathe?

Once you've developed the right mindset and begun to notice which thoughts are harmful for you and which ones serve you, you'll be more enthusiastic and optimistic throughout the day even when faced with challenges. While you'll still feel down from time to time, especially during the toughest times, you will find it easier to spring back. Most importantly, despair won't cling to you, and you won't yearn for the brief euphoria that comes from stress eating. The rule you should always keep in mind is this: "Success is 80% psychology and 20% strategy." By practicing mindfulness, you will become more aware of your thoughts and beliefs and, as a consequence, you will no longer be reactive to them. Instead, you will regain the power to change them into beliefs that will serve your goals. Keep reading and you will find out more on how to transform your life.

Slow Down for Bigger Woes

Now, there may be instances in which things get too intense and you'll find it difficult to use these quick methods. Fortunately, there is a simple mindfulness strategy that you can instantly apply to release tension and relax – it's called *Freedom through Gratitude*.

Here's how you do it:

- Leave behind whatever is triggering your negative thought patterns.

- Look for a quiet place, preferably somewhere you can be alone for a while.

- Recognize the main negative thought that has manifested in your mind.

- Now, begin to breathe in a deep yet relaxed way.

- Each time you exhale, imagine the thought moving out of your body.

- Once you're beginning to feel a little lighter within, focus on gratitude.

- Fill your mind with things for which you're thankful.

As you practice this technique, focus on all the small things you can be grateful for: your eyes, hands, healthy organs, roof over your head, job that gives you money to buy food and clothes, your parents, people around you… The list can go on endlessly. What is important here is that you don't need amazing achievements, luxurious goods, the partner of your dreams to show gratitude and understand how happy and blessed you already are. Learn to be grateful for everything you've got. I really love this beautiful quote by an anonymous author that really captures what matters in life:

"A good life is when you assume nothing, do more, need less, smile often, dream big, laugh a lot and realize how blessed you are for what you have."

The more accustomed you become to releasing the negativity and replacing it with positive thought patterns, the more success you will have in all areas of your life. Be grateful for your body. Appreciate it. Value it. Take good care of it, and it will pay you back by becoming the strongest and best-looking temple you've ever dreamed of.

To find out how, keep reading…

CHAPTER 5

The Stress and Metabolism Connection

As you probably already know first, stress can either make you gain or lose weight. The hormone responsible for these changes is cortisol. Cortisol boosts your metabolism and stimulates your appetite. So even if your body burns more calories when you are stressed out, all that cortisol in your bloodstream also makes you eat more to compensate for it. Increased cortisol levels tend to produce stomach fat. So, if you want cortisol to stop making you fat, you have to relax. Take a deep breath. Live a peaceful life. Let your calories burn naturally.

The Connection Between Stress and Metabolism

If you are stressed out, either emotionally or physically, your body is flooded with cortisol and epinephrine. This process is referred to as the fight-or-flight response. Cortisol taps into energy reserves, converting your bodies stores of fat, glucose, and protein into usable fuel. When this happens, your body burns calories and your metabolism increases.

Cortisol is also as a catabolic hormone, however, which means that it breaks down muscles to use for energy. Stress may increase your ability to burn calories initially, but it also causes your body to lose muscle. If you continually get stressed out, your metabolism will decrease over time. Long-term chronic stress is dangerous to your health.

The Connection Between Stress and Appetite

At first, you may have a weak appetite because you are stressed out. However, if this stress goes on, you may become ravenous. Your epinephrine levels can help prevent hunger initially, but if you still continue to feel stressed out, your cortisol levels will increase and you will get hungrier over time.

When you experience these cortisol-induced hunger pangs, you may crave for foods high in sugar and fat. While these choices seem comforting, they are actually bad for your health. According to researchers, these kinds of food make you feel better by triggering the areas of your brain responsible for your emotions and stress. People tend to crave for unhealthy "comfort foods" whenever they are feeling stressed.

Stress and Weight Gain

If you experience chronic stress often, you will lose muscle and increase your appetite for unhealthy foods. If you give in to your unhealthy cravings, your belly size and body fat will increase. In addition, cortisol in your body will cause your insulin resistance to increase. This typically happens when cells no longer stay responsive towards the insulin that brings in sugar from the blood. As a result, there would be an increase in your insulin and blood sugar levels.

According to a study published in Cell Metabolism in 2012, there is a connection between obesity and high insulin levels. Insulin resistance is caused by chronic stress, which can also boost your risk of having type 2 diabetes. In order for you to be able to manage your stress levels effectively as well as boost your metabolism naturally, you have to exercise. You should consult your doctor if you have any exercise routines in mind. See to it that you are physically fit to perform the exercises.

Vigorous exercises are perfect for fighting against stress — however, if you have been sedentary for a long time, suddenly performing vigorous exercises can be bad for your body. Thus, you need to start with lower intensity exercises to help your body adjust to your new routine. You can start by brisk walking for thirty minutes every day of the week.

As you continue to exercise, your body gets used to the activity. When you feel that you are ready and brisk walking is no longer a challenge, you can start jogging and then running. You can also practice yoga, tai chi, and meditation to improve your metabolism further. They are not only effective in fighting against stress, they are also effective in increasing the number of calories that you burn during rest.

CHAPTER 6

Relaxation and Burning Calories

If you are like most people trying to lose weight, you are likely working hard for it. While hard work is essential for achieving your goals, it can be disadvantageous when it comes to losing weight. This is because being hardworking can make you highly stressed out. When you are in a heightened state of anxiety, tension, fear, or force, your metabolism dramatically changes.

Some people claim that they actually lost weight when they went on a vacation and ate more food. Others claim that they did not lose any weight despite following a strict diet. This may seem impossible. However, recent studies have found that metabolism and digestion are correlated with relaxation. When you relax, your nervous system goes from chronic sympathetic dominance (responsible for your fight or flight reaction) to parasympathetic (controlling relaxation and calming feelings). Your frame of mind changes your metabolism to an extent that you can eat more yet still lose weight.

Remember that cortisol is the primary hormone released in response to stress. In studies that involved monkeys and rats subjected to stress, weight gain was caused by increased cortisol levels. They gained weight even though they were given normal amounts of food.

Just like in people, weight gain can result in spite of a low-calorie diet and an exercise program. If you are often stressed out, you will gain unnecessary weight no matter how frequent you exercise and even if you eat less. In addition, chronic stress can increase your insulin production. Insulin is another hormone that is connected to weight gain. Each time there is an increase in blood sugar, insulin is produced by the pancreas. This insulin lowers the level of glucose in the blood by instructing the body to store extra dietary carbohydrates as fats. Insulin also tells the body to stop releasing stored fats.

Insulin resistance is a condition in which insulin production and chronic stress become highly problematic. During this condition, the levels of blood sugar stay high in spite of increased insulin production. This occurs because the target cells of this hormone become unresponsive. If you compound this process by consuming foods that are high in carbohydrates, you will gain weight faster.

In other words, you will not lose weight if you constantly worry about it, if you follow a forced diet, and if you do not believe that you can have a healthy body. If you practice negative self-talk, you will hinder yourself from achieving your weight loss goals. Even if you consume fewer calories, you will still gain weight if you are stressed because of the increased insulin and cortisol in your bloodstream. Stress reduces your thermic efficiency or your capacity to burn calories and use stored fat as fuel.

If you want to relax and burn calories, you should give yourself a break. You can take a week off work or go on a trip. Do the things that you love and indulge in your hobbies. Sleep more, go for a walk, play sports, or read books. You can also practice meditation and yoga. Yoga is especially a great way to relax and lose weight because it is a form of exercise. Through yoga, you can burn about 100 to 450 calories per hour.

CHAPTER 7

The Psychology of Eating

A huge number of people squander the benefits of good nutritional habits because they make some fairly common mistakes. What's interesting, however, is that they know what they have to eat—they are educated on good nutrition, and they have a clear idea on what they need to do with regard to their health. Yet, in spite of all this knowledge, they still do not do what they know they should do.

Simply understanding how much you have to exercise or knowing what you need to eat does not guarantee that you will achieve weight loss. You have to act on what you know in order for it to work for you. Simply put, what you eat is just half of good nutrition. Who you are as an eater is the other half. The way you feel, think, and believe about stress, awareness, pleasure, and relaxation – all these affect your eating habits and metabolism in many ways.

Pondering on Psychology

Experts believe that the body and mind profoundly affect each other. They're basically saying that you have the power to change your health status without altering your diet, but simply having to change who you are as an eater.

Do you pay attention to what you're eating? Do you fully appreciate the food on the table? You might be missing out on the eating experience, and thus your mind doesn't send signals of satiety and satisfaction. Of course, the psychology of eating also encompasses matters involving your mental and emotional states, as well as your beliefs. These have an effect on how your body processes food. For example, as we've discussed in the previous chapter, if you're stressed out, you're less likely to metabolize your food efficiently.

All these pieces of information highlight the need to learn to watch out for psychological traps in eating. With the right level of awareness (or, in other words, by being mindful), you'll know how your mind is leading you to poor dietary choices or preventing you from burning the food you eat. That means you will have enough time to think about what you're going to do (or what you're currently doing) – and you will have the chance to make the right decision, or to put a stop to your harmful actions.

Matter of Stress Awareness

Stress can make you gain weight, but relaxation can make you lose it. It is amazing how fear, stress, anger, anxiety, negative self-talk, and judgment can result in a physiological stress response in your body. You generate more insulin and cortisol when you harbor negative thoughts and stress. As a result, your body stores more weight and fat. It also stops building muscle.

Your stress levels literally affect your capacity to burn calories. However, when you smile more often, breathe more deeply, and feel more at ease, your body goes into a physiological relaxation response. You achieve your optimal metabolism day in and day out. On the other hand, if you are anxious, your mind limits the capacity of your body to lose unnecessary weight.

Being happy is the best way to aid digestion. When you feel stressed or anxious, you may experience heartburn, stomachache, cramping, and gas. During stress, the body shifts into a fight or flight response, which is useful during life threatening situations. Once your stress response gets activated, your digestive system shuts down. Your energy gets directed towards survival. So, even if you eat healthy food, you still do not get all the nutrients you need if you are not in a relaxed state.

Be Present, Avoid Overeating

Overeating is a common problem. However, it is actually a very simple concept. Some people think that they overeat due to a weak willpower. They think that they cannot control their appetite, and it is why they cannot lose any weight. The truth is that they do not have a problem with their willpower. They are simply overeaters who do not eat when they eat. What does this mean?

When you do not eat when you eat, you are not completely present during your meal. You are not fully aware of how it tastes or how it nourishes your body. Your brain misses out on a vital phase of nutritional experience, which involves satisfaction and taste. Your brain either thinks that it did not eat enough or it did not eat at all. So, you think that you are hungry and you eat more than you are supposed to. If you want to avoid overeating, see to it that you increase your presence and awareness during mealtime.

Also, there is this misconception that when you eat quickly, you boost your metabolism. The truth is that eating slowly helps you boost your metabolism. When you eat quickly, you put stress on your body. Keep in mind that humans are just not biologically designed for high-speed eating. If you eat quickly, you put your body into a physiologic stress response. This, in turn, causes decreased nutrient assimilation, digestion, and calorie burning rate. Conversely, it causes increased appetite and nutrient excretion.

When you slow down, you improve your nutritional metabolism. You also get to taste your food better, which heightens your satisfaction. You need to increase your pleasure in eating to enjoy it more. You do not have to eat more of the food. You just have to take some time to appreciate its taste, presentation, and overall quality. Pleasure actually catalyzes a relaxation response as well as fuels assimilation and digestion. What's more, you get the chance to chew your food more carefully. You can make sure that you are able to digest it properly.

On Emotions and Thoughts

With regard to emotional eating, you have to remember that you are human, meaning that you're an emotional being. You have feelings, such as happiness, sadness, anger, and fear among others. This makes you prone to emotional eating, wherein you eat according to how you feel. More often than not, people eat to comfort themselves in times of despair or sorrow. You have to get rid of this habit and replace it with something healthier.

For example, whenever you are feeling down, you should go out for a jog. Being outdoors lets you breathe in fresh air. Jogging is great way to raise your heart rate and exercise your body. Both of these are good for you because they relax you and make you feel good. More importantly, they keep you away from your refrigerator and prevent you from reaching for a tub of ice cream. When you eat comfort foods, you feel good at first. Eventually, however, you start to regret your actions because you know that your body and health will pay for it in the end.

Furthermore, you have to get rid of your toxic and unhelpful nutritional beliefs. Do not be like those people who think that food is an enemy. Food is not your enemy. If you become fat, it is not the food's fault. It is your fault. If you harbor these beliefs, you will have an unhealthy relationship with food. So, you must change the way you think about food.

CHAPTER 8

Binge Eating, Compulsive Overeating, Emotional Eating

Binge eating and compulsive eating are unhealthy eating habits. You have a problem when you feel compelled to eat even when you are not hungry or you cannot stop eating when you have already had enough. These eating disorders are actually more common than bulimia and anorexia.

According to Belin and Fairburn, experts on eating disorders, about one in every two people aiming to lose weight have binged in the previous month. One in every four people trying to control their weight were diagnosed with binge eating disorder.

Binge eating disorder refers to the eating disorder wherein an individual is not able to prevent himself from eating huge quantities of food, usually in a short period of time and while in a mindless state. People who have been diagnosed with binge eating disorder often feel out of control with their eating habits.

Compulsive overeating refers to the condition in which eating becomes out of control and seems more like a food addiction. Those who overeat compulsively are not able to control their eating, which in turn makes them gain weight. They tend to struggle with weight control and often have unexplainable cravings. At times, they may overeat large or small quantities of food.

Emotional eating is when you "eat your feelings". When you are sad, overjoyed, excited, or depressed, you may eat junk food to feel better. People who describe themselves as emotional eaters tend to succumb to comfort food as a way to cope with their negative emotions.

In any case, binge eating and compulsive overeating are very similar. People who are classified in both groups believe that they do not have full control of their eating habits. They believe that they do not have enough willpower and that they eat for comfort instead of for their physical needs.

According to experts, binge eaters and compulsive overeaters tend to:

- Eat faster than normal
- Eat past their point of fullness
- Eat even when they are not hungry
- Eat in secret
- Feel guilty after eating too much
- Feel that they are not normal

- Feel that they are taken over by an unexplainable presence when they eat

- Try to compensate for their overeating by purging or dieting

Compulsive eating can affect both men and women, regardless of their age or race. Nonetheless, women are more inclined to seek help for their condition than men. This is because women tend to be more concerned about their physical appearance and the way their eating habits contribute to it.

Most compulsive eaters start to eat compulsively after dieting for a certain period. They also tend to describe themselves as kind people who put the needs of others before their own. They often have a hard time expressing or identifying their needs. They may also lack clarity with regard to how they feel or what specific emotions they are experiencing. Because of this, they are not able to properly deal with their feelings. In addition, they tend to have low self-esteem and feel the need to be approved of by their peers.

Food Addiction

Some people are addicted to food. They crave certain types of food and give in. They are not able to stop even when they are already full if they like the taste of the food. Overeaters and food addicts use food to achieve feelings of satisfaction. They often try to stop their food addiction, but just like other types of addicts, they often experience a relapse. Also, just like drug and alcohol addiction, food addiction can interfere with your life and put a strain on your relationships.

Stress Disorder and Negative Body Image

More often than not, people who binge eat or eat compulsively suffer from stress disorders and/or negative body image. Their stress can even stem from the disorder itself. When you overeat, you may blame yourself for your actions, and this can make you stressed out afterwards. When you are ashamed of your behavior and you try to hide it from other people, you may become stressed out too. Again, your problems with overeating can make you more prone to overeating. It becomes a never-ending cycle.

Those who binge eat also tend to dislike the way they look. Their negative body image causes them to feel the need to eat less. Because they constantly worry about their physical appearance and the way other people think of them, they become stressed out. Also, their constant worry of eating more than they are supposed to make them stressed out even further. Such feelings of stress cause them to binge eat or eat their feelings.

Then, there are others who just give up on themselves. They think that they are already fat, so why should they attempt to change their eating habits? They think that it is hopeless for them to lose weight and be healthier. Some of them do not even exert effort simply because in their minds, their case is hopeless already. If you have a negative body image, you have to address that issue. You have to improve your self-esteem and start accepting yourself for who you are. Once you successfully address it, you will be able to deal with your bad eating habits.

Deeper Emotional Problems

Sometimes, however, there is more to simply having a negative body image. Some people have far deeper emotional issues that they need to resolve. In these cases, their binge eating or compulsive eating is a sign of a much deeper psychological problem.

Binge eaters who are severely overweight have a greater risk of developing anxiety disorder, depression, and alcohol addiction. Compulsive eaters who practice dangerous weight control practices (such as using laxatives or forcing themselves to vomit) tend to have suffered traumatic events in their childhood. These people need to receive the necessary treatment in order to address their underlying issues. It is only when these issues have been resolved that they can start focusing on their poor eating habits.

Treatment

The first step of treatment should be consultation with a professional who knows about eating disorders and has the ability to determine what type of compulsive eating the patient has. A complete eating history can help the medical professional to determine the challenges and events that predisposed the patient to the problem. Such assessment also pinpoints whatever keeps the patient stuck.

Treatment is supposed to be directed towards both emotional and physical factors, which maintain the unhealthy relationship of the patient with food. This treatment should depend on the results of the assessment. Keep in mind that the treatment for compulsive overeating is more than merely having a positive relationship with food. The patient has to be attended to as a whole.

The medical professional or therapist should help the patient effectively deal with feelings or emotions, eat comfortably in different situations, manage social situations well, sleep properly, overcome stressors, deal with personal relationships, improve self-esteem, say 'no' to unhealthy foods and toxic people, and be healthier.

Keep in mind that antidepressants are not ideal to be used for treating eating disorders like binge eating and compulsive overeating. If you use prescription drugs to treat your condition, you will be at risk of experiencing unpleasant symptoms once you stop taking medication. Appetite suppressants are not recommended either. Just like prescription drugs, they can make you experience unpleasant symptoms in the long run.

The best way to treat your binge eating or compulsive overeating is through therapy. If you have other issues such as phobia, then you may use prescription drugs. You have to consult your doctor to know about the most recommended treatment procedure.

CHAPTER 9

The Implications of Hormonal Imbalances

Hormonal imbalances are a huge epidemic in the United States. Those 35 years of age and above typically suffer from it. Unfortunately, many fail to understand what the problem really is. In short, a hormonal imbalance stems from the body's need to have its hormones at balanced levels, especially in relation to one another. These hormones serve as regulators of and triggers for various physiological processes, as well as affect the production of other chemicals and neurotransmitters that are vital for healthy functioning.

If one of these signaling molecules drops or increases in availability, one (or more) functions of the body may fail to proceed properly. For example, women who experience severe menstrual cramps possibly have too much estrogen. In conventional medicine, this is resolved by giving progesterone – a hormone that suppresses estrogen. Sleeping disorders and chronic acne are other common examples of concerns caused by incorrect hormone levels.

Implications on Weight Gain

So, what does this have to do with your quest to lose weight? There are four hormones that, if not kept at proper levels, could increase your tendency to gain pounds. The first among these is leptin, which is produced by fat cells. This hormone serves as an alarm, telling your brain that you're already full. The problem begins, however, when you eat so much that your body finds it necessary to store the excess as fat.

When you have too much fat in your system, leptin increases significantly and your body develops a resistance towards it. By failing to effectively detect signals of satiety from this hormone, you'll find it harder to feel full during meals, which means overeating becomes much more likely. If this remains unresolved (or if you allow it to manifest in the first place), you will be gaining more pounds despite feeling more deprived.

Estrogen is another hormone that's linked to weight gain. It's among the main reasons why women tend to store fat in certain parts of their body (such as in their hips and breasts). So, as you'd expect, an abnormal abundance of this hormone will force your body to store as much fat as possible; likewise, given that your system is focused on fat storage, it will be much harder to shed the pounds you've gained.

Here's one important thing you need to keep in mind when it comes to estrogen – while it is commonly referred to as the female sex hormone, it's definitely present in both men and women. Also, know that there are different reasons why estrogen levels rise excessively. Among these are insufficient amounts of progesterone, and exposure or consumption of estrogen-like substances (some meat products, or soy contain these hormone analogs).

As discussed previously, insulin is a major hormone that serves as a glucose regulator. Whenever there's too much sugar in your system, insulin acts to lower its amount – there's a downside to that though, which comes in the form of increased fat deposits. The hormone doesn't flush glucose out of your body—it stores it for future use. While that may seem economical, insulin is actually harmed by excess amounts of fat and becomes less effective in doing its job.

Last among these hormones is cortisol. Since we have discussed it in length in the previous chapters, there's no need to discuss it further here. Just keep in mind that whenever you're faced with a stressful situation, your body releases cortisol into the bloodstream. This prepares you for the "fight or flight" response, and one way of doing that is by adding to your visceral fat. While this serves as an energy source whenever necessary, it's unlikely that you'll need it.

The Mindfulness Approach

Many would surely agree that hormone replacement therapy can be an effective means of dealing with some hormonal imbalances. However, according to research, those taking in hormones are at a higher risk of heart disease, blood clots, breast cancer, and stroke. This leads more people to turn to bio-identical hormone replacement therapy, which is supposedly safer but still comes with a myriad of risks.

What risks exactly? For one, bio-identical hormones do not undergo standardized safety evaluations. Another is that these substitutes are prepared in different ways, given the lack of FDA-approved guidelines to follow. So, quality can't really be guaranteed either. The manner in which they're prescribed (and their doses determined) can be rather problematic, as some rely on saliva hormone testing alone—an inaccurate approach, given that hormone levels can shift temporarily.

Fortunately, there's another way of battling (or preventing) hormonal imbalance—and it's by practicing mindfulness. Through mindfulness (and by engaging in the meditative practices that it entails), you become more aware of the present. You will be able to stop yourself from overeating, you'll get to make better dietary choices, and you'll find it easier to keep yourself calm during tough situations.

By being less likely to eat excessively, you become less at risk of developing problems with leptin and insulin resistance. It's probably best to provide an example at this point. Let's say you've decided to eat mindfully and so, you eat slowly and appreciate food's texture, flavor, and aroma to the fullest. Since you get utmost pleasure from every bite, it wouldn't take as much to reach that necessary level of satisfaction to feel full.

Having too much estrogen will not be much of a concern either, as long as you're well aware of what you're eating—after all, you will be able to stay away from food that possibly contains substances that mimic the hormone. You'll have to remember that mindful eating isn't just about the experience—it's also about knowing more about what you're putting into your mouth for the purpose of appreciation. Where is it from? How was it grown? How was it made?

For example, if you've been eating pre-packed bacon rather frequently, you will begin to ask questions about how it's processed. That would lead to you seek answers as you shop for more the next time around, and it's likely that you'll finally realize how unhealthy your choice is. If there's no guarantee that it's organic or grass-fed, you've most likely been ingesting estrogen-like substances the whole time. From this realization, you begin your search for something better.

As for cortisol, the calming effect of mindfulness should keep you protected from chronic stress—keeping the hormone's level in check. Here's another example—you're been in meetings the entire afternoon and you begin to feel your anxiety creeping in. With the right mindfulness techniques though (for example breathing exercises), it will be easier to keep stress at a minimum. Likewise, with mindful eating, you reduce your risk of eating too much just to gain instant gratification.

CHAPTER 10

Happy Exercise vs. Stress Exercise

You already know that exercise is good for your health. It reduces your risks of diseases such as type 2 diabetes, stroke, and cancers. It also helps you control your weight and be in a lighter mood. However, you should know that exercise can also have the opposite effect. Instead of making you happier and healthier, it can make you stressed out and gain weight.

There is this true story about two people: a 48-year-old lawyer, and a stockbroker who is about the same age. Both are women. The lawyer was trying to lose weight but she was unsuccessful. She has already undergone numerous tests, but the doctor could not find anything wrong with her. She was on a diet and she ran every day. She was actually a marathon runner who should be able to easily lose fifteen pounds.

In spite of her efforts to lose weight, she remained fat. Her diet was deficient in fat, calories, and protein. This put her body in a survival response and slowed down her metabolism. Also, she ate quickly, did not feel satisfied with her meals, and rarely ate nutritious food. She starved herself to lose weight. Her doctor advised her to eat more and relax. She did as she was told, but she gained six pounds.

The other woman, the stockbroker, was in a similar situation. She could not lose weight, even though she has already tried everything. The doctor gave the same advice to the stockbroker: eat more proteins and fats, eat slowly, and eat more often. The woman gained four pounds. Surprisingly, she was not upset. She was still positive about losing weight. That was when the 'aha' moment came in.

Intense exercise, especially when done far too frequently and not coupled with a proper diet regimen, could force your body to enter what experts call starvation mode. In this mode, your body stores fat and prevents muscles development. It can also elevate your insulin and cortisol levels, as well as produce inflammatory chemicals. Why does this happen? It's a biological means of self-preservation—you've been exercising too rigorously that you're body thinks it's in danger.

Most people believe that the more often you exercise, the more weight you can lose. Conventional wisdom has taught them that weight is all about gaining and burning calories. In reality, however, exercise is not black and white. According to Dr. Kenneth Cooper, who has done research at the Cooper Aerobics Center, doing thirty minutes of low-intensity and moderate-intensity exercises three to four times a week is best for fitness, health, and weight maintenance.

The doctor asked the stockbroker why she ran marathons. She replied that she liked to run and she wanted to be fit. Eventually, she revealed that she really did not like running. She only did it to punish herself because she was fat. The doctor discovered that the fearful thoughts of the patient caused her to have physiologic stress response. Her fight or flight state was escalated by a form of exercise that was not right for her body. Because of this, she had more stress chemistry. In spite of her attempts to lose weight, she was not able to achieve her goals because she did not like running.

So, the doctor asked the stockbroker to stop running marathons and do something that she really likes instead. The woman took yoga and dance classes. After three months, she lost eight pounds. She was pleased with the results, especially since she no longer has to run marathons to lose weight. She enjoyed the physical activities that she did. This only proves that exercising can backfire on you if you do not use it the right way.

When Exercise Makes You Stressed Out

Exercise generally elevates the mood. It can help fight against anxiety and depression too. In some cases, however, it can do the opposite – just like what you have just read above.

If you really dislike a particular exercise routine and yet you still do it anyway, you will not reap the benefits that you hope to reap. Instead, you will put yourself under an emotional duress. The stress of forcing yourself to exercise will put you in a bad position.

The stress caused by exercise is evident in studies that involved animals. In certain experiments, the animals were forced to exercise, causing them to feel stressed out. Their stress levels were measured using physiological and behavioral markers. The researchers found out that their cortisol levels were increased.

With regard to the direct impact of voluntary and forced exercises on emotional resilience and anxiety, scientists from the Center for Neuroscience at the University of Colorado at Boulder conducted a study that can prove this theory. Their study lasted for six weeks.

First, they gathered male rats that liked to run and allowed them to exercise for as long as they wanted to. This was the first group of rats. Then, they monitored the pattern and duration of the rats' exercise. Just like humans, they exercised in slow and fast intervals.

Next, the scientists forced other rats to exercise. The rats were placed in mechanical and lockable wheels. They had to run even if they did not want to. The scientists made these rats mimic the pattern of the first group of rats. Their daily mileage was similar to that of the first group.

The scientists then introduced a third group of rats. They were placed on mechanized treadmills with a steady and even pace. They were not able to control the distance or speed of their running. Finally, the scientists used a fourth group of rats to serve as the control group. These rats stayed sedentary.

The scientists exposed the rats to stress. They placed them in unfamiliar cages to see if their levels of confidence or anxiety would change. The rats that scurried or froze in dark corners were regarded as unsettled and highly anxious. Those that ran in the treadmill and stayed sedentary were found to be the most anxious rats. On the other hand, the rats that ran on wheels were found to be resilient. They were able to bounce back from stress easily.

From the study, you can see that even forced exercise can have positive results. However, unlike the rats that used the wheels, the rats on the treadmill were not able to start and stop. They were forced to run continually at a steady pace. They were not able to have intervals in their exercise.

According to Benjamin Greenwood, an integrative physiology professor at the University of Colorado, forced exercise can still increase stress resistance. This is perhaps why people are still able to lose weight when they are forced by their trainers to work out. However, the intervals between running and walking can have an added impact on the emotional effects of a workout. This is why speeding up and slowing down when biking or running can make you feel more satisfied.

CHAPTER 11

Mindful Eating

Mindful eating is all about eating with attention and intention. It is a mindfulness practice that can help you improve your relationship with food. When practicing it, eat with the attention needed to enjoy and notice your food, along with its effects on your health. Also, eat with the intention of taking care of your body.

In essence, mindful eating is more than just eating slowly and without distraction. It also encompasses awareness of emotional and physical cues, learning to meet your needs more effectively, recognition of non-hunger eating triggers, choosing to eat for nourishment and enjoyment, eating for safety and satisfaction, and using food to live a vibrant life.

Most of the people who struggle with food mindlessly react to unexamined or unrecognized triggers, feelings, and thoughts. They repeat their actions continually and feel that they do not have any power to change anything. Through mindfulness, you can increase your awareness of your eating patterns without any judgment. You can also create a space between your actions and triggers.

For instance, each time you feel an urge to eat, you should pause for a while and ask yourself if you are really hungry. Observe your thoughts thoroughly and be careful how you respond. Rather than react mindlessly, you have to be responsible for your response. Mindful eating helps you break habitual or automatic chain reactions so that you can discover choices that can work better.

By asking yourself if you are hungry, you can understand what, when, why, how much, and how you should eat. You will also learn where you have to invest your energies. If you want to achieve your fitness and weight loss goals, you have to be aware of your eating decisions.

Why do you eat? What drives your eating cycle? When do you want to eat? When do you think about food? When do you finally decide to eat this food? What do you eat? What option do you go with? How do you eat? How do you get the food into your body? How much food do you eat? Where do you invest the energy that you consume? What happens to the fuel that you have?

Principles of Mindful Eating

Your relationship with food reflects your attitude towards yourself and your environment. Mindful eating can bring awareness towards your actions, feelings, motivations, and thoughts. It can also bring awareness towards the roots of your contentment and health.

Keep in mind the following principles of mindfulness:

- It deliberately pays attention in the present moment in a non-judgmental manner.

- It encompasses both external environments and internal processes.

- It is about being aware of your physical sensations, thoughts, and emotions during the present.

- With practice, it cultivates the possibility of setting yourself free from habitual and reactive patterns of acting, thinking, and feeling.

- It promotes choice, acceptance, balance, and wisdom.

When you practice mindful eating, you let yourself become more aware of the nurturing and positive opportunities that are available through the preparation and selection of food while simultaneously respecting your inner wisdom. You use each and every one of your senses as you select foods that are nourishing and satisfying. You acknowledge responses towards food, such as liking, disliking, or being neutral about it, without any judgment. You become aware of the satiety and hunger cues that guide your choices.

You can say that you are a person who practices mindful eating when you acknowledge the fact that there is no wrong or right way to eat, but rather there are different degrees of awareness that surround your experience with food. You practice mindful eating when you accept that every person has a unique eating experience; and directing your attention towards eating on a moment-by-moment basis is the first step in this practice of mindfulness. You practice mindful eating when you are able to make choices that are supportive of your wellbeing and health. Furthermore, you are aware of the interconnection of the Earth, humans and other living creatures, and the impact of food selections on different systems.

CHAPTER 12

Mindful Breathing

Mindful breathing is effective in helping you deal with chronic stress. Chronic stress negatively affects your cognitive functioning, physical health, and emotion regulation. You have to know how to manage stress properly so that you can foster health, wellbeing, and success.

There are long-term and short-term strategies you can use to manage your own stress levels. Mindfulness is effective in enhancing cognitive functioning, such as performance, memory, and concentration. It can also improve emotion regulation and resilience, self-awareness, and relaxation.

For your short-term strategy, you can apply mindfulness in the present moment—in the here and now. At random moments throughout your day, pause for a while and breathe deeply. Do this several times each day. When you shift your attention from what is going on around you and you take a mindful breath, you can reduce your stress levels.

In essence, you have to focus, observe, and refocus. You have to focus on breathing deeply. Then, you have to observe that deep breath, and refocus if necessary.

Keep in mind that chronic stress can affect your brain just like too many running applications affect your computer. If you open several applications and run them all at once, your computer will slow down. It might even crash. The same thing can happen to your brain. Your brain will slow down, and it may no longer be as functional.

When you deal with a lot of mental tasks, you reduce the processing speed of your brain and trigger frustration. You become highly stressed out. When you pause briefly, you focus on just one task to clear the mind. Such action helps your thinking brain to catch up with your emotional brain. This allows you to refocus better and come up with decisions that are more rational.

When are the ideal moments to pause and take mindful breaths? As much as possible! You have to practice mindful breathing every day. You can do it before you do normal tasks such as before you answer the phone, while you wait for your laptop to boot, and before you start or end a meeting. You can also practice mindful breathing while you walk to the kitchen, before you reply to an email, before you eat or drink, and upon waking up in the morning and before going to bed at night.

Just like physical fitness, mental fitness requires training. You have to train your mind if you want it to get stronger. You have to exert effort and time. You have to practice and persevere to get the results that you want. As you continue to practice it, the easier it gets for you.

Here are more tips on how you can successfully practice mindful breathing:

Look for a peaceful and comfortable place. Position yourself in a way that is comfortable for you. You can sit on a chair or cross your legs on the floor. You can sit on a small cushion to stay balanced and comfortable. Sit up straight. Your back has to be kept upright, but do not make it too tight. Place your hands on your lap and lightly place the tip of the tongue against the bridge of the palette..

Keep your body relaxed the entire time. Observe your posture and position. Observe your body and your weight too. Allow yourself to relax as you stay seated down. Observe your body sensations. How do you feel while you sit down on the chair or floor? Observe the way your body touches the surface of the chair or the floor. Think about their connection with each other. Keep all areas of your body free from tension or tightness. Take deep breaths.

Take your attention towards your breathing. Observe the natural flow of your breath. Feel it coming in and out of your body. There is no need for you to do anything with your breathing. Do not make it short or long. Just let it flow naturally. Observe where you feel the breath within your body. It may be in your abdomen, throat, nostrils, or chest. Find out if you can feel the sensations of your breathing. Take one mindful breath at a time. As soon as a breath ends, take the next one. You have to be in a continuous flow.

As you practice mindful breathing, you may notice your mind starting to wander. Your mind may start harboring various thoughts. Do not worry, most beginners usually experience this. As you continue to practice mindful breathing, the better you get at it. Each time you notice your mind wandering, carefully bring it back to your focus. Forgive yourself for not being perfect. You can utter the words 'wandering' or 'thinking' quietly in your head as you gently bring back your attention to your breathing.

For five to seven minutes, you have to stay like this. Observe your breath silently. You may get lost in your thoughts for some time, but you can always bring your attention back to your breathing. After several minutes, observe your body again. This time, pay attention to your entire body. Allow yourself to relax more deeply. Appreciate yourself for your efforts. Then, you can end your mindful breathing session for the day.

CHAPTER 13

Mindfulness Mini Habits for Weight Loss

Weight loss requires discipline. If you are determined to lose a few pounds, you have to change your lifestyle. This includes the way you eat, exercise, and think. You also need to adopt new habits that can benefit your health. The following are some of the mindfulness mini habits you can adopt to lose weight safely and naturally:

1. Differentiate between appetite and hunger

Knowing their difference is crucial for mindful eating. Remember that hunger is actually a physiological condition in which your body informs you that it is time to eat. Hunger is controlled by your hypothalamus. Your hunger signals are not the same as those of other people—however, it is common for a lot of people to find themselves grouchy and lightheaded when they are hungry. You can also say that you are hungry when you feel your stomach growling.

Appetite is different from hunger. It is not a physiological condition, but rather a strong desire. It is typically affected by the thought, sight, and smell of food. Your appetite does not have anything to do with your hunger. You may feel a craving for a certain type of food without actually feeling hungry. You may already be full and yet still want to eat more. In short, it is your appetite that keeps you eating.

Here's the question though—how does one distinguish between the two? It's not that complicated actually. Just take note of physiological signs, ranging from a drop in your energy levels to a growling stomach. If you've been noticing those and you're getting the urge to eat something, then it's likely that you're genuinely hungry. On the other hand, if your eagerness to eat is fueled solely by thoughts regarding taste and preference, it's probably your appetite talking.

Another way to know whether you're feeling true hunger is checking how long it has been since your last meal, as well as taking into account how much you've eaten. If it has been a couple of hours or if you've only had a light breakfast and you're feeling hungry, having a snack should be fine – after all, you probably need it to keep your energy up.

You may also try a simple test to find out whether you're faced with hunger. Think of one particular food that you don't find tasty at all—something you won't really choose if you're dining in a buffet-type restaurant. Let's say you've chosen Brussels sprouts. Now, whenever you're feeling the urge to eat, ask yourself this question: "Am I so hungry that I'd eat a serving of Brussels sprouts?" If you answered yes, then it's practically guaranteed that you're hungry. Make no mistake here, it's not about starving yourself to death (this wouldn't be a healthy approach at all) but about being aware of your sensations in the body and allowing some time to actually recognize between true hunger and appetite.

2. Use the hunger scale when you eat

Once you become more accustomed to differentiating between hunger and appetite, you're ready to try using the hunger scale. It's basically a means of rating your levels of fullness and hunger. On most hunger scales, the number 1 is an indication for starvation, while the number 10 is an indication for having overeaten. Here's a sample that should get you started (feel free to tweak it a bit to better fit your own unique ways of responding to fullness and starvation):

- 1 – You're starved. You feel very weak and your stomach is grumbling.

- 2 – You're so hungry that you can no longer concentrate. You feel irritable.

- 3 – You're uncomfortable as your stomach just won't stop grumbling.

- 4 – Stomach discomfort (due to acids) annoys you from time to time.

- 5 – You feel satisfied, but you know there's still space in your tummy.

- 6 – You're full and you don't have any urge to eat further.

- 7 – You're a bit too full, leading to mild discomfort.

- 8 – You're so full that you feel bloated.

- 9 – You've eaten so much that you need to loosen your clothes.

- 10 – You feel nauseated due to the sheer amount of food you ate.

When you use the hunger scale, you have to eat before you feel so hungry and you have to stop before you become so full. You will know that it is time to stop when you feel satisfied after having a meal and yet you're still able to go brisk walking. Likewise, you have to start eating before you become ravenous. By doing all these, you'll be able to keep your caloric intake at just the right level – without really paying attention to labels and literally counting values.

3. Don't classify food as bad or good

You will only set yourself up for failure if you classify foods as bad or good. Why will that happen? When you eat food classified as bad, you end up feeling guilty. When you feel guilty, you harbor a negative emotion, which can cause you to be stressed out. When you are stressed out, you experience a hard time losing weight. You also become prone to a variety of illnesses.

So, instead of classifying foods as bad or good, you can instead classify them as healthy and not-so-healthy. For instance, broccoli is a healthy food. When you eat lots of broccoli, you nourish your body. Candy, on the other hand, is a not-so-healthy food. It lacks the nutrients that your body needs but it gives you energy nonetheless. Since it is not so healthy, you should not eat it every single day. However, you can still have some candy once in a while.

You must not restrict yourself when it comes to food, so feel free to eat a wide variety. If you tell yourself that you can never have a certain type of food, you will only crave for it more. For example, if you are trying to lose weight, you may tell yourself that you can never eat cake again. However, the more you try to avoid it, the more you will think of it. You will only get stressed out thinking about it and not being able to have it.

Allow yourself to have a slice of cake once in a while. When you feel free to eat anything, you will no longer feel stressed. This would let you boost your metabolism and lose unwanted weight. Then again, you need to have self-control. While you can eat cake, you must know how much you should have. You can have a slice to satisfy your craving, but you should not eat the entire cake because doing so is unhealthy.

If you stress too much over what you eat, you take the joy out of eating. You no longer experience pleasure with food. Hence, you should refrain from thinking too much about following a certain diet or buying food products that are low in calories or are non-fat. Learn how to enjoy food. Be kinder to yourself when it comes to your dietary habits.

4. Don't hide behind food

A lot of people tend to eat because they feel sad, depressed, or anxious – this is what experts refer to as emotional eating. Those who engage in it use food as a means to feel better. However, giving in to comfort food will not do you any good in the long term. In the short term, you will feel better. Then, you will start to feel guilty and realize what you have done.

You can prevent this from happening by simply acknowledging your feelings. When you feel sad, accept it. Do not eat something to try to hide it. Instead, think about why you are feeling sad. What is the root cause of such feeling? Remember that when you mask feelings like these, they will just get worse. If you do need a quick endorphin boost though, it's better to shift your energy and attention to a more productive activity. You can take a walk, jog, read a book, or knit.

Even though it's healthier to engage in such activities whenever you're feeling down, angry, or afraid, you still need to resolve the issue or face whatever it is that's triggering your emotions. If that's not possible (such as if the problem has already lapsed yet it still bothers you), just be honest with yourself—pinpoint the root of your concern and reframe your thoughts about it. Be grateful for the things that have gone the way they should, and seek the silver lining.

Note that emotional eating isn't just about feeling the need to enjoy something sweet when something goes wrong. The way you feel about something you've experienced in the past—or still go through on a daily basis—could have created poor eating habits as well. For example, before you go to work in the morning, you feel this need to stop by the donut shop —if you fail to do this, you feel anxious, as if something has gone wrong or as if you're left defenseless.

Try to pinpoint these patterns by increasing your awareness as you go through each day. Once you have identified them, ask yourself whether they're really necessary—determine whether you'll really be put in a vulnerable spot if you choose not to do them anymore. Also, try to be mindful of the triggers, and think of better ways of handling them—once again, reframing your thoughts and focusing on the positive should prove to be useful in this endeavor.

CHAPTER 14

Practical Mindfulness Exercises – Step-by-Step Easy to Follow Mindfulness Routines to Lose Weight

Mindfulness exercises are designed to help you avoid going on autopilot. When you go autopilot, you perform the tasks but fail to notice their essence. You also become judgmental because you give in to notions that were influenced by your past experiences. Through mindfulness exercise, you can effectively deal with the challenges that come your way with a clearer mind and a calmer demeanor. You develop a conscious mind that sets you free from unhelpful and limiting thought patterns.

No matter how hectic your schedule is, you must always find a way to exercise. With this being said, you should not only exercise your body, but your mind as well. The following are some highly recommended mindful exercises that you can do to keep your body in shape:

1. Mindful Breathing

You can do this exercise while sitting down or standing up, whichever feels more comfortable for you. You can also do it anywhere as long as it is peaceful, quiet, and clean.

a. Begin by inhaling and exhaling slowly. Each cycle should last for about six seconds. Inhale through your nose and exhale through your mouth. Allow your breath to naturally flow in and flow out of your body.

b. Let go of all your thoughts for about a minute. Stop thinking about the chores that you have to do or the projects that you have to finish. Just let yourself stay still.

c. Observe your breathing. Focus on how your breath goes into your body and fills your entire system. Observe the way it goes out of your mouth when you exhale.

2. Mindful Observation

Practicing this exercise helps you connect with the beauty of nature. Oftentimes, people become so busy that they forget to notice and admire their surroundings. With this exercise, you can stop for a while and see the beautiful things around you.

a. Select a natural object. You can choose anything you see around you. You can even focus on the moon or the clouds.

b. Focus on the object. Observe it for one to two minutes. Relax yourself as you concentrate. Look at the object as if it is your first time seeing it.

c. Explore every part of it. Let yourself be consumed by its presence. Connect yourself with its energy as well as its purpose or role in the world.

3. Mindful Awareness

Through this exercise, you can strengthen your appreciation and awareness of simple tasks as well as their results.

> a. Think of the things that happens to you on a daily basis. It can be anything, from opening your windows to cooking breakfast. Think of the normal things that you do.
>
> b. When you do that particular activity, such as opening your windows, you should stop for a while and start to be mindful. Think of where you are at the moment and how you feel. What do you see when you open the windows? Do you see your garden with beautiful flowers? Do your windows open to a magnificent view of the city?
>
> c. Appreciate what you see. Be grateful that you have hands to open the windows and eyes to see what is beyond them. Be grateful that you have an opportunity to experience a moment like that.
>
> d. Select a touch point that resonates with you each day. Rather than go on autopilot with your daily activities, you should stop once in a while to cultivate mindful awareness.

4. Mindful Listening

Through this exercise, you can train your ears to listen without being judgmental. More often than not, what you hear is influenced by past experiences. When you listen mindfully, you are able to achieve a present awareness that is neutral, allowing you to listen to sounds without any preconception. The main idea behind this exercise is to merely listen and become entwined with the music without any judgment.

>   a. Choose a song or type of music that you have never listened to in the past.
>
>   b. Close your eyes as you listen to the sound or song. Ideally, you should use a pair of headphones so that you can listen to it better.
>
>   c. Refrain from judging the song or music by the title, artist, or genre before you even play it on your device. Ignore the labels and allow yourself to immerse in the sound naturally.
>
>   d. Explore each aspect of the song or music track. Let go of your feelings of dislike if the music is not your type. Give yourself permission to immerse in the sound waves.

5. Mindful Immersion

Through this exercise, you can find contentment in the moment. It allows you to escape for a while so that you do not get carried away by the things that you do on a daily basis. Instead of desiring to finish a task anxiously, you become able to feel every moment of it, fully experiencing it like never before. The main idea behind this exercise is to help you become more creative and allow you to discover new experiences with familiar routines.

a. Do something that you do routinely, such as cleaning the house.

b. Pay attention to each detail of your task. Instead of treating it as a normal chore, you should create a whole new experience out of it. Observe each aspect of the action.

c. Feel the motion. Become the motion. Sense which muscles you use when you clean the floors. Find a more efficient way to clean the windows.

d. Rather than constantly thinking of finishing the task, you have to be aware of every step. Immerse yourself completely in the process. Take the simple activity beyond your routine. Align yourself with it mentally, spiritually, and physically. Eventually, you will no longer feel anxious about cleaning. You may even enjoy it.

6. Mindful Appreciation

The main idea behind this mindfulness exercise is to help you become grateful and appreciative of things that seem to be insignificant in your life. These are the little things that support your existence, but you rarely get a chance to notice because you focus on pursuing bigger experiences or acheivements.

a. Select something that you do not notice every day, but is important in your life. Electricity, for instance, powers your lighting fixtures and electrical appliances. Water quenches your thirst and is good for your health. Your eyes allow you to see everything around you.

b. Find out how that particular thing supports your life and makes it better. How does it work? Where did it come from? How can it benefit others?

c. Imagine your life without this particular thing. How is your life different without it? Do you think that it is easier or more difficult without it?

d. Notice its finer and more intricate details. Study it further.

e. Choose other things that you tend to ignore and yet are very important. Think of how they interconnect with one another. Think of the roles they play in your life.

f. Each day, you should choose at least five things that you tend to neglect. List them down in a notepad. Appreciate them more. Cross them off your list, and then choose more things.

CHAPTER 15

Losing Weight – What Works and What Doesn't Work (Debunking Myths)

If you are serious about losing weight, you should know the strategies that work and the ones that do not. This way, you can go straight to the strategies that work and no longer waste time on the ones that do not.

What Works

1. *Drink lots of water*. Drink water before you eat a meal. It can make you feel fuller, so you end up eating less. Drinking a glass of water before mealtime can reduce your intake of calories.

2. *Stop drinking calorie-filled drinks*. Sodas and canned juices are full of calories. You may think that the fruit juices you see in the supermarket are healthy, but they are not. Canned or bottled juices are high in sugar and calories. If you are not fond of drinking water because it is tasteless, you can add a few drops of lemon or put some cucumber slices in your water bottle.

3. *Make lifestyle changes*. There is a popular myth that when you exercise consistently, you will not gain weight. This is not true. If

you want to be healthier and have a better appearance, you have to make the right food changes in your lifestyle. Combining exercise with the healthy, nourishing food can give you most satisfying and lasting weight loss effects.

Keep in mind that your metabolism slows down with age. So, the older you get, the more cautious you have to be of your diet, exercise regimen, and overall lifestyle.

What Doesn't Work

1. *Not having snacks*. A lot of people have this misconception that when you eat more, you gain more weight. Thus, they limit the amounts of food that they eat. However, you have to realize that snacking is not always a bad idea. In fact, having snacks throughout the day is good for your metabolism. You can eat between meals.

When you feel your stomach growling, you can have a light snack. Having snacks help you stay full and avoid overeating or binge eating. Many dietitians recommend having five small meals per day, including snacks in between major meals.

Then again, you should still choose the snacks that you have. As much as possible, you should go with healthier options. Refrain from snacking on cookies, chips, and candies. If you feel like having something sweet, you can have some fruit slices instead of a bar of chocolate. If you are craving for something salty, you can grab a handful of salted nuts instead of potato chips.

2. *Staying away from fast food all the time.* You already know that when you restrict yourself from certain foods, you will only have a stronger craving for them. This is why you have to let yourself indulge in fast food once in a while. You can eat a cheeseburger and some fries. Just don't overdo it. Also, whenever you are in a fast food restaurant, you may want to order the better choices. You can get a salad as an appetizer. You can also choose grilled chicken instead of fried chicken. Soft tacos are also better than their crispy counterpart.

3. *Do not be afraid of carbohydrates.* Not all carbohydrates are bad. Some of them are good for your body, such as vegetables and fruits. These foods contain fiber, which is helpful in digestion. However, you should steer clear of processed carbohydrates such as white flour and sugar. If you need to sweeten your coffee, use date nectar, which contains no sugar and is loaded with manganese, carotenoids, phytosterols, and metabolizing minerals. You can also use honey or stevia.

CHAPTER 16

Optimizing Your Results with Supplements, 7 Minute HIIT

Supplements can help ensure that your body gets all the nutrients it needs. So, aside from eating whole grains, fruits, and vegetables, you should also take high quality supplements as part of your diet.

Supplements

1. *Garcinia cambogia extract*. It is small, green, and looks like a pumpkin. Its skin has hydroxycitric acid (HCA), which is a powerful ingredient. According to studies, this supplement inhibits fat-producing enzymes in your body as well as increases your serotonin levels. It can help reduce your cravings. It can also help you lose a few pounds over a few weeks of usage. Although it does not have any serious side effects, it can make you experience mild digestive problems. Consult your doctor before you take it.

2. *Hydroxycut*. It contains ingredients that are said to be effective for weight loss. Some of its main ingredients are plant extracts and caffeine. According to a study, it can help you lose up to 21 pounds within three months of usage. Since it contains caffeine,

you should refrain from using this supplement if you have caffeine sensitivity. Otherwise, you may experience jitteriness, anxiety, irritability, diarrhea, tremors, and nausea.

3. *Green coffee bean extract.* It comes from raw coffee beans and contains chlorogenic acid and caffeine, which are both effective for weight loss. It also contains powerful antioxidants. The caffeine it contains can help you burn off fat faster while the chlorogenic acid can slow down the carbohydrate breakdown in your gut. In addition, this supplement can help you lower your blood pressure and blood sugar levels. However, you should not take it if you are allergic to green coffee beans. You may also experience diarrhea due to the chlorogenic acid present.

High Intensity Interval Training (HIIT)

If you want to lose weight quickly and effectively, you may want to try HIIT which stands for High Intensity Interval Training. HIIT is a style of exercising which involves short intervals that you do with almost maximum effort. Those bursts of intense exercises usually include: sprinting, biking, skipping rope, knee highs, followed by short recovery periods such as walking.

In order for HIIT to work for you, you have to be intense during your workout. You have to train your body to go into work anaerobic mode so that it can be more efficient at using energy. As you progress into your HIIT sessions, the fat burning potential of your body gets better.

HIIT became really popular amongst people who want to lose weight and improve overall endurance, as it never allows your body to adjust to one intensity level. Your body receives 'a shock' needed to start using the fat as fuel for your workout.

HIIT also has an afterburn effect. While at rest, your body continues to burn calories for the next 48 hours. You can be sitting on the couch and you will still be melting fat away. The short yet intense bursts of exercise allow you to build muscle and improve your resting metabolism rate. This is why a 20-minute HIIT workout is better than a 1-hour treadmill workout.

Keep in mind that intensity is the key. You must work out at a seven to eight on your rate of perceived exertion scale for every interval. When you perform strength training exercises, see to it that you focus on your form.

How about VO2 max? What is it and why do people keep bringing it up when they talk about HIIT? The VO2 max of your body is its measurement for the maximum amount of oxygen that it is allowed to use. This VO2 max is a primary factor in identifying your level of endurance.

According to researchers, you have to reach 80 to 100% of the VO2 max of your body when you perform HIIT if you want to get maximum benefits. You know that you have reached your Vmax level of exertion if you can no longer take in as much air as you want. Simply put, if you can still communicate with another person while you work out, you have not reached your Vmax level yet.

During HIIT, your goal is to reach and maintain your Vmax level. You have to move fast for long periods. When your breathing is labored, you have to hold your speed for a certain period. You need to have intensity. Do not jog; sprint instead.

Once you reach your Vmax level of exertion, you have to sustain it. Keep in mind that the effectiveness of your HIIT workout depends on how much time you spend at attaining your Vmax level of exertion.

Here is an example of 7 – Minute HIIT Workout that will melt your belly fat that you can easily do at home:

Instructions: Do each exercise at high intensity for 30 seconds followed by a 10-second rest. Repeat entire circuit up to 3 times.

During the session, bring all your attention to the present moment. Relax your muscles and as you do the exercises, observe your bodily sensations and your breath. Be as mindful as you can. Don't judge: "Oh, it's too hard, I can't do it" or "I have no energy, I am too tired". Observe those thoughts coming and let them pass. Bring your attention to now.

1. Start off from **JUMPING JACKS**. Do these for a total of 30 seconds. It will warm up your body. Rest for 10 seconds. Repeat the cycle two more times.

2. **WALL SIT:** Stand with your back against the wall. Place your feet about two feet out in front of you, hip distance apart. Bend your knees and slide your back down the wall until your knees are at 90-degrees angle.

Make sure your knees don't fall in on the midline of your body or sway outward. Hold this position for 30 seconds. Rest for 10 seconds. Repeat the cycle 2 more times.

3. **PUSH UP:** Begin in a plank position with palms spread out evenly, shoulders over your wrists and legs out behind you. Pull your belly button in. Keep your back straight. As you lower and exhale, bend your elbows outward to the sides. Hold at the bottom before you raise back up. Do as many reps as possible in 30 seconds and then rest for 10 seconds.

4. **CRUNCHES:** Lie down and bend your knees. Plant your feet on the floor. Put your palms behind your ears. As you exhale, pull your abs in and lift your upper body. Inhale as you lower back down. Keep your chin down to keep your neck from straining. Do maximum reps in 30 seconds. Rest for 10 seconds. Repeat the cycle 2 more times if possible.

5. **SQUAT:** Stand with your head facing forward. Place your feet shoulder width apart. Extend your hands straight out in front of you to help keep your balance. Sit back and down like you're sitting into an imaginary chair. Lower down. Your thighs should be parallel to the floor and knees over your ankles. Press your weight back into your heels, keep your body tight. Push through your heels to bring yourself back to the starting position. Do as many reps as possible in 30

seconds and then rest for 10 seconds. Repeat the cycle 2 more times.

Do these exercises minimum three times a week for the next 4 weeks and the results will amaze you.

After your workout, do 10 minutes of stretching and 5 minutes of relaxation. To relax, simply lie down on the floor and focus your attention on your breath. Don't wrestle with your thoughts. Allow them to come and go.

CHAPTER 17

Balancing Your Hormones

When you are under stress, your adrenal glands produce cortisol (stress hormone). Too much cortisol blocks estrogen. When your cells receive less estrogen, you get less serotonin (so called hormone of happiness). If you have low serotonin, you can suffer from sleep problem and agitation, making you cranky and irritable. Furthermore, when serotonin drops your brain releases norepinephrine (another stress hormone), makes can your heart pound, give you hot flashes, spike your blood sugar, and increase your breathing rate. And before you know it, you're in this vicious cycle and you don't know how to stop it. You start to think in black and white. Hormone imbalance can also start with high stress, which then causes the hormones to get out of whack. Sometimes we don't know which came first, the hormone imbalance or the stress.

When your hormones are imbalanced, you will have a hard time maintaining your ideal weight. This is why you have to make sure that your hormones are well-balanced. Here are some tips to help you balance them naturally:

1. Practice Mindfulness Meditation

New research from the Shamatha Project at the University of California suggests that focusing on the present moment can significantly help lower cortisol levels. Mindfulness meditation releases serotonin, responsible for maintaining mood balance and oxytocin, responsible for our bonding and romantic relationships. It also increases our melatonin levels, which is a hormone that controls our sleep and wake cycles. Another amazing benefit of meditation is the increase in dopamine production, which is the hormone responsible for our focus, memory and cognitive skills.

2. Eat Healthy Fats

Your body needs different types of fats to produce hormones. These fats are essential in producing hormones and keeping levels of inflammation low. They also improve metabolism and help with weight loss. You can get healthy fats from: avocados, butter, coconut oil, extra virgin olive oil or walnuts.

3. Take Adaptogenic Herbal Supplements

These herbs are ideal supplements. They promote hormone balance as well as protect your body against various diseases. They are effective in boosting immune function, fighting against stress, improving thyroid function, lowering cholesterol levels, reducing depression and anxiety, reducing brain cell degeneration, supporting adrenal gland function, and stabilizing insulin and blood sugar levels. Some of the most popular are tulsi (holy basil), rhodiola and ashwaganda.

4. Consume Omega-3 Fats

The cell membranes in your brain are largely composed of omega-3 fatty acids. They are vital for the communication among cells. According to researchers, omega-3 fatty acids reduce pro-inflammatory responses and prevent hippocampal neuronal loss. You can get omega-3 fatty acids from flaxseeds, wild fish, chia seeds, grass-fed beef, and walnuts.

5. Take care of your Gut Health

You need to have a healthy diet in order to avoid leaky gut syndrome, which is a condition that affects your digestive tract and causes hormone problems. You can develop leaky gut syndrome if undigested food particles leak from your gut to your bloodstream. When this happens, you can suffer from inflammation that causes disease and negatively affects your endocrine glands (adrenals, thymus, thyroid, etc.). Those who have this condition tend to lack probiotics, which are healthy bacteria that boost the production of leptin, insulin, and ghrelin in their guts. This is why you have to stay away from processed foods, hydrogenated oils, sugar, and gluten, as they can damage your digestive system. Instead, you should eat fermented vegetables, high-fiber foods, sprouted seeds, kefir, and bone broth.

6. Throw Away Toxic Beauty, Body Care, and Kitchen Products

You should avoid using products that contain dangerous chemicals such as parabens, DEA, sodium lauryl sulfate, and propylene glycol. Instead, you should use natural products that contain shea butter, castor oil, coconut oil, and essential oils. You should also avoid using plastic bottles and containers as well as aluminum cans because of their toxic bisphenol A (BPA) content. Instead, you should replace them with stainless steel and glass.

7. Get Sufficient Amounts of Sleep

Your body generally needs seven to eight hours of sleep. When you lack sleep, the natural circadian rhythm of your body is disturbed and you can suffer from hormonal imbalance. Take note that your hormones function on a schedule. The hormone cortisol, for instance, has the highest level in the morning and the lowest between midnight and 4 am. This is why people who do not go to bed early tend to have issues with their sympathetic flight or fight stress response. If you want to maximize your hormone function, you should get to sleep no later than 10 PM.

8. Do Not Use Birth Control Pills

You can find safer alternatives. Birth control pills raise your estrogen to dangerous levels. Taking them puts you at risk of many health complications. Long term use of these pills can cause increased risks of breast cancer, uterine bleeding, heart attack, stroke, and blood clotting. It can also cause breakthrough bleeding between your cycles, increased blood pressure, migraines, back pain, nausea, mood changes, breast tenderness, liver tumors, and weight gain.

CHAPTER 18

Great Nutrition Strategies that Will Speed Up Your Metabolism

Your weight loss can depend on how good your metabolism is. By metabolism we understand the process by which your body converts what you eat and drink into energy. Since you are aiming to lose weight, see to it that you follow these tips:

1. Eat Lots of Protein During Mealtime

When you eat, you boost your metabolism rate for several hours. This happens because of the thermic effect of food (TEF), which is caused by the caloric activity necessary to absorb, process, and digest nutrients. Protein makes your TEF rise. It also raises your metabolic rate by 15% to 30%. When you eat protein, you feel more satiated and you do not overeat. You also prevent experiencing a drop in your metabolism because protein prevents the loss of muscle, which often occurs when you go on a fad diet.

2. Drink Oolong or Green Tea

These beverages can increase your metabolism by 4% to 5%. They can also turn fats into free fatty acids, which can increase the fat burning ability of your body by 10% to 17%. They are low in calories, so they are also ideal for weight loss and maintenance.

3. Eat Spicy Food

Foods that contain capsaicin, such as peppers, can increase your metabolism. According to a study, consuming capsaicin at appropriate doses can help you burn an additional ten calories for every meal.

4. Lift Weights

Your muscles are more metabolically active than fats. So when you build muscle, you boost your metabolism. This allows you to burn calories even while resting. You should lift weights in order to retain muscle and prevent a drop in your metabolism. Usually, people experience a drop in their metabolism when they try to lose weight.

According to a study of forty-eight overweight women who consumed 800 calories a day, those who performed resistance training were able to maintain muscle mass, strength, and metabolism. On the other hand, those who only performed aerobic exercises as well as those who did not exercise at all lost muscle mass and slowed down their metabolism.

5. Stand Up More Than You Sit

Sitting down for long periods every single day is not good for your health. Sitting does not burn as many calories as standing. In fact, you can gain more weight if all you do is sit around.

According to a study, standing up for an entire afternoon while at work can help you burn an additional 174 calories. This is why some companies provide standing desks to their employees.

CHAPTER 19

Healing Nourishment

Maintaining a healthy lifestyle requires that you have a healthy eating plan or a balanced diet. The Dietary Guidelines for Americans states that a healthy eating plan puts emphasis on fruits, whole grains, vegetables, and low-fat or fat-free dairy. It includes lean meat, fish, poultry, nuts, beans, and eggs. It is low in trans and saturated fats, cholesterol, added sugars, salt, and cholesterol. It also stays within your calorie requirements.

When it comes to healing nourishment, you should consider a wide variety of foods. You may be surprised to find out that some of the foods you thought were purely evil can actually give you benefits.

For instance, even though experts recommend staying away from canned food products, you may still eat canned fruits. Fruits are good for you, whether they are frozen, dried, fresh, or even canned. You can eat canned apples, bananas, mangoes, pineapples, and kiwis among others. However, you should look for canned fruits in water instead of syrup.

Just like fruits, you can also eat canned vegetables and herbs. You can pan fry them or use them as a side dish. However, you should opt for canned vegetables that do not have added cream sauces, salt, or butter.

Foods that are high in calcium are also good for you. You do not have to stick with fat-free and low-fat free milk though. You can also have yogurts, but make sure to forego the added sugars. You can enjoy yogurts in different flavors for dessert.

You do not have to give up on your favorite comfort foods either. The key to healthy eating is balance. You can still eat junk food and fried foods, but you have to do it in moderation. You have to balance them with your healthier food choices.

Do not eat your favorite comfort foods every day. If you are so used to having them daily, you can train yourself to cut back little by little. At first, you can cut back to just once a week. Then, you can have your comfort food once every two weeks. Eventually, you can just have it once a month. Gradually cutting back on your comfort foods allows your body to get used to not eating them.

You should also eat your favorite comfort foods in small amounts. You can use a smaller plate or bowl when you eat cake or ice cream. You can also cut your chocolate bar in half. This way, you will not be tempted to finish the entire cake, chocolate bar, or tub of ice cream.

You can also go for a lower-calorie version. Some brands offer lower-calorie versions for people on a diet. You can also prepare your own food by using lower-calorie ingredients. For instance, you can use non-fat milk, light cream cheese, less butter, and fresh tomatoes and spinach for your macaroni and cheese instead of whole milk, full fat cheese, and butter.

CHAPTER 20

Building Lifelong Mindfulness Habits

You're now fully aware of how mindfulness can help you lose weight. Surely, you also know that its beneficial effects are more encompassing than most people think. Well, in this bonus chapter, we will talk about mindfulness habits that should improve your life in the long term.

HABIT #1: Keep a Gratitude Journal

As we've pointed out several times in this book, it's important to be grateful for the things you have. Showing gratitude even for the smallest things makes you more aware of your blessings and keeps you from focusing on life's most discouraging moments. Instead of only occasionally appreciating the good, however, it would be best to keep track of it. You'll be overwhelmed as you look back at how fortunate you are in the past days, months, or years.

To start your very own gratitude journal, just get your favorite pen and a sufficiently-thick notebook (you're going to keep it going for years, after all). There are no set rules on how to write this kind of journal, but it does help to follow a few basic guidelines, such as:

- Do your best to maintain a regular schedule, but don't be too eager to put something in your journal. For example, you may choose to write thrice a week, with a day in between each entry. Even if you have had a great day, as long as it's not time to write, don't add an entry. This way, the feeling of gratitude would last longer and you'll learn to appreciate it more.

- If you're having a hard time thinking about something to write down, consider the fact that good things aren't limited to nice gestures and selfless deeds directed towards you. It's also about the misfortunes you've avoided or prevented even if simply through sheer luck. As they say, some of the best things happen unintentionally.

- Don't hesitate to be specific. Being as detailed as possible allows you to fully appreciate your gifts. Vividly remembering the who, what, when, and how of each event you're grateful for will be more heartwarming once you begin reading past entries than seeing a general statement like, "I'm thankful for my family."

- Don't be afraid to repeat things. Good happenings in life don't have to be completely unique, so do not force yourself to keep things fresh whenever you're writing in your journal. Remember that you're not trying to engage readers with whatever you're writing—after all, you're the only one who's supposed to read your journal!

HABIT #2: Break from Technology

Among the newest mindfulness habits is engaging in the occasional digital detox. This entails distancing yourself from most modern devices (specifically those that eliminate the need to interact with people firsthand), albeit only for a limited time. As you'd expect, this kind of habit will give you the chance to appreciate those around you. It also brings an opportunity to see what the environment offers in terms of amazement and relaxation.

Once you're ready to start this new mindfulness habit and bring your awareness to new heights, just follow these steps:

- Determine your limits, or know how much you'll be able to distance yourself from technology. Let's be realistic. Due to various circumstances, not everyone can simply choose to refrain from communicating with long-distance clients or faraway family members. This is why you'll have to set boundaries on how disconnected you'll be. For example, you may choose to stay away from social media but keep your phone line active.

- Once you're done defining your limits, it's time to ponder upon the duration of your detox. Much like staying away from all forms of technology, suddenly disappearing from the online world for an entire month could be disastrous to some. So, given this issue, most people choose to schedule their digital detox during weekends. Even two days should be enough to relieve yourself from the stresses of interconnectivity.

- At this point of the planning stage, you'll have to get in touch with a few friends and ask if they would be willing to accompany you in your tech-free journey. You could try scheduling a trip that lasts for the entire duration of the detox, but that's not always going to be an option. Instead having dinner and staying unplugged throughout the brief gathering should suffice—what's important is that they understand and support what you're doing.

- Once you've planned all activities involving other people, it's about time that you think of things to do during your alone time. You could try exploring the outdoors solo (of course, safer routes are recommended), but the typical choice is reading a good book. This allows you to relax and really listen to your thoughts.

- When everything's set, you're ready to finally begin your digital detox. Be sure to stick to the duration and boundaries you've set, but feel free to change your itinerary a bit—especially if there are unexpected happenings (such as your friends not being able to come, or the weather suddenly becoming worse).

- At the end of your endeavor, be sure to reflect on the things that have happened. Take note of anything that you've learned throughout the experience, and ask yourself whether you really need all the gadgets you have in your home. Also, it is at this point that you should consider making your detox a habit. Think of the challenges you've faced and the possibility of setting a fixed schedule.

Do either of these (or both) and soon, you'll notice great improvements in your awareness. You will be able to appreciate life's many wonders, and you will appreciate those around you even more. Most importantly, these lifelong habits should help further your personal development—now and in the years to come.

CHAPTER 21

10 Steps Mindfulness-Based Program that Will Melt off Fat Forever

Knowing the key concepts in mindfulness-based weight loss is important—and if you need to recall a specific piece of info, you'll always have the option to re-read certain chapters of this book. Sometimes though, you might prefer a more straightforward guide. Well, this step-by-step program should satisfy that need. It will also serve as a template once you begin to add awareness to your life.

STEP 1: Make the Decision

As with any weight loss endeavor, you'll have to be committed to pursuing the goal—and you'll need to know when to begin. If you're wondering whether you should start tomorrow or the week after, you have to change your mindset. It must begin in the soonest possible time, which is now. Don't worry about the pressure that comes with the changes. After all, you're going to rely on a technique that emphasizes the need for calm and appreciation.

STEP 2: Set Your Expectations

Once you've made the decision, you need to come up with expectations. Be sure to create realistic ones to prevent yourself from developing a negative body image. Do not aim for a specific figure or a particular weight. Simply target improvements that will make you feel healthier and happier in a holistic manner. Write down all your expectations on a piece of paper and be sure to keep it somewhere safe.

STEP 3: Be Mindful as You Shop

If you really want to lose weight and maximize the potential of mindfulness, you will have to prepare food on your own—at least most of the time. As you shop for ingredients though, be aware of the differences between choices. Ask questions such as "Where is this from?" or "How was this made?" to pinpoint the healthier options. It won't hurt either to spend a bit more time reading the labels. As much as possible, pick food items that are additive-free and unprocessed.

STEP 4: Do Meditative Cooking

To truly melt off fat forever, you will need to prepare your meals on your own. No, it's not some boring task that you can assign to someone else. It's actually an opportunity to practice mindfulness, or to have additional time to meditate. Put your entire consciousness into the act of cooking. Notice everything that happens, one by one. Make it a point to do every step in the most thorough and correct way possible. Soon, you will begin to look forward to the experience.

STEP 5: Engage in Mindful Eating

On your next meal, and in the meals that follow, remember to observe the basics of mindful eating. Savor each bite and take note of details such as texture, flavor, and aroma. Appreciate the way in which the food was prepared—think about how the ingredients were grown or raised, and consider the effort involved in creating something so scrumptious. Since mindful eating requires you to eat slowly, don't hesitate to allocate at least half an hour for each dining activity.

STEP 6: Live a Life of Mindfulness

If mindfulness brings so much more to mealtimes, it's only appropriate to assume that it would greatly enhance other aspects of your life. In this step, you should begin to integrate mindfulness in many of your day-to-day activities. For example, during your commute, be aware of those around you. Notice the small details, such as the sounds and sights. Simply put, you'll have keep your senses awake at each passing minute.

STEP 7: Keep Your Stress in Check

It's only to be expected that not everything you'll see is brimming with positivity. Also, challenges are part of life, so it won't be realistic to focus on being happy all the time. It's for this reason that you'll need to practice breathing exercises. Whenever you feel stressed, seek a quiet enclosed space and breathe—let go of your stresses with each exhale. Well, even if you're not that stressed, doing some breathing exercises during your breaks should help in keeping calm all day.

STEP 8: Do the Right Exercises

Another important part of this step-by-step program is getting enough physical activity. Do note, however, that there are exercises that only lead to more stress, and there are those that improve your physique as well as keep the endorphins flowing (for more details on this, refer to Chapter 10). When you have finally chosen an appropriate exercise based on your preference and activity level, be sure to make it a part of your routine.

STEP 9: Show Gratitude Each Day

Keeping your stress at a minimum is an integral part of this program. Likewise, it's important that you stay positive in all situations. So, aside from doing mindful breathing and engaging in the right exercises, you must practice gratitude. Each night before you sleep or right after waking up, recall all the good things that happened to you recently. Be grateful for those who helped you, and for the things that turned out well.

STEP 10: Reflect on Your Progress

If you've been accomplishing all the previous steps so far, progress is only to be expected. You may reflect on your progress either weekly or monthly, although the latter should be better if you're just starting. During your checks, however, don't merely focus on whether you've lost weight (you shouldn't even count)—the most important question to ask is, "Do I feel better?" Don't hesitate to find out if some of your expectations have been met.

CONCLUSION

I hope this book was able to help you learn more about mindfulness and how it can help you lose weight. As you know by now, losing weight isn't just about counting calories and doing exercises—it's about having the right mindset towards food and towards your chances of accomplishing such a transformative pursuit. Mindfulness is a powerful way to change your views and adopt healthier habits one day at a time. So, what are you waiting for? It's time to start practicing mindfulness and reaping its rewards!

Thank you!

Before you go, I'd like to say thank you for purchasing my book.

I really hope this book will help you implement mindfulness techniques and strategies you have learnt into your life to effectively manage stress and achieve more inner peace.

Now, I would like to ask for a small favor. Could you be so kind as to leave your honest review?

Each review is worth its weight in gold as it's of tremendous help to increase the book's visibility and help the author reach more readers. Reaching 50, and then 100 reviews, is a vitally important milestone for every author.

If you're strapped for time, even just one or two sentences will do.

Thank you so much,
Sarah

MORE BOOKS BY SARAH

Mindfulness. Simple Techniques You Need to Know to Live in The Moment and Relieve Stress, Anxiety and Depression for Good (Mindfulness Book Series, Book 1)

Mindfulness for Social Anxiety Relief. Learn How to Regain Control of Your Life and Overcome Social Anxiety, Fear, Worry and Self-Criticism Forever (Mindfulness Book Series, Book 2)

Depression. 22 Ways They Don't Want You To Know To Naturally Cure Depression For The Rest Of Your Life

Leaky Gut No More. 12 Proven Ways to Heal Leaky Gut Naturally. Boost Metabolism and Lose Weight Permanently – Look and Feel Great. (The Gut Repair Book Series, Book1)

GAPS Diet. 30 Nutrient-Dense Recipes to Alleviate Chronic Inflammation, Repair the Gut Wall and Regain Energy (The Gut Repair Book Series, Book2)

Fermented Vegetables: Top 30 Delicious Recipes for Fermented Vegetables and Probiotic Foods that will Restore your Optimal Gut Health (The Gut Repair Book Series, Book3)

Printed in Great Britain
by Amazon